Kurt Hunter's

Simple Little Book of Marionettes

With illustrations by Steve Mark

Table of Contents

1 Acknowledgements

My fascination with marionettes started when I saw a performance by Tony Urbano and his company as a teen. I didn't realize at the time just how high the bar was set by that performance. In the years that followed I was very lucky to increase my understanding of marionettes in workshops, classes and interactions with some incredible puppeteers. In roughly chronological order I would like to acknowledge David Syrotiak Sr., Margo Rose, Jim Gamble, Bob Kramer, Dug Feltch, Jim Rose, Albrecht Roser, Phillip Huber, Bernd Ogrodnik, Alice Gottschalk and Ronnie Burkett. My gratitude also goes out to the countless other puppeteers who have inspired me.

Nothing helps you figure out what you think you know like teaching. I sincerely thank all of the people who have attended the workshops and classes that I have taught over the years. Their interest, attention and questions have helped me refine my understanding of marionettes and improve the way that I present the information.

Supporting everything that I have done with marionettes in the last few decades has been the love, feedback and insights of my wife Kathy. I am incredibly lucky to have this joyful, intelligent and gifted woman at my side.

2 Introduction

This little book will not teach you how to build or operate marionettes. However, it will attempt to help you understand some fundamental ideas that are very important when building and operating marionettes. After years of helping others get started with marionettes I have a good idea of where beginners frequently stumble and what can be confusing at first. This book will hopefully help you avoid some of the common mistakes, so you are more likely to have a successful start with this amazing form of puppetry.

A lot of people think that marionettes are complicated. Like many things, marionettes are simple until they aren't. If you are just starting with marionettes, I think it is a good idea to start with simple. Albrecht Roser, the German marionette master, would start students with the simplest marionette, a wooden ball on one string. A student could spend hours (and I have) exploring what is possible with the simplest marionette.

I once heard the legendary musician Bobby McFerrin say in an interview that if he was teaching piano lessons he would spend the first couple of weeks focused on middle C, just exploring what can be done with that one note, rhythmically, dynamically and so one. Simple is a good place to start.

3 How many strings?

How many strings does a marionette need? Well, that depends on your marionette.

One String

Let's say the story you are telling has a magic turnip. The turnip isn't a little person that looks like a turnip. It's just a turnip that doesn't really need to do anything special. One string may be enough for this marionette.

Two Strings

Marionettes are great at flying and swimming, so many marionette shows include underwater scenes. These underwater scenes usually have some fish that are essentially two dimensional. They don't need to do much beyond swimming towards the surface or swimming towards the sea floor. For these marionettes two strings should be enough.

Three Strings

You've made a very simple bird marionette with outstretched wings and no moving parts. You want it to soar and bank. For maximum control of this one piece marionette, you need three strings.

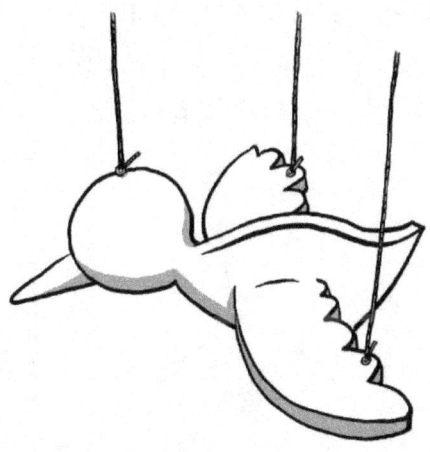

The idea that you have maximum control of a single object by controlling three points (with three strings) is called **"Three Point Control."** Think about a stool with three legs. You can set it on any uneven surface and it will be stable. However, a stool with four legs is only stable if placed on a flat surface. On an uneven surface, three of the legs will touch the ground and one leg won't. It will wobble between two legs. The same is true with strings. Four strings on a single object will generally not add control and can make the object wobble between two of the strings.

More Strings

If your marionette has any moving parts you'll need more strings, but how many more?

Let's say you've built a bird with moveable wings. Each wing is attached to the body at two points with cords, so the wings can move up and down easily. The body has two strings to the head and one string to the tail. How many additional strings will give you full control of a wing? You just need one string for each wing.

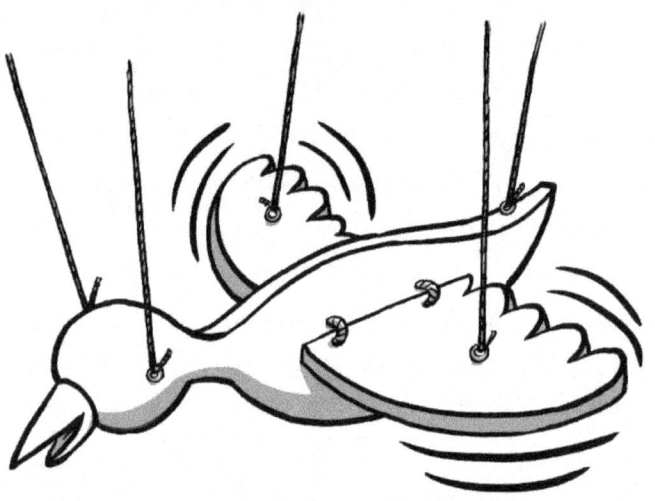

As you work with this marionette you discover that you can't get it to lean left and right very far, because the strings on either side of the head are so close together. You decide that you would rather have greater control of the head than of the body.

You give the bird a simple cord neck joint and add a string to the front of the body. The two strings on the body give you two point control of the body like the fish mentioned earlier.

The two strings on the head allow the bird to look up and down and side to side. Because the attachment to the body will also affect the orientation of the head, two head strings are all you need.

Nine Basic Strings

A marionette with more moving parts will require more strings. Extrapolating from the previous examples it is clear that the number of strings necessary for "maximum control" of every moving part of a marionette of a human character is quite large. However traditional marionette stringing doesn't attempt to support "maximum control" of each part of the marionette. Decisions have to be made about what movement will and won't be possible.

Traditionally these necessary compromises lead to a marionette with nine strings. The "nine basic strings" on a marionette are:

- Two head strings (HE)
- Two shoulder strings (S)
- One lower back string (B)
- Two hand strings (HA)
- Two leg strings (L)

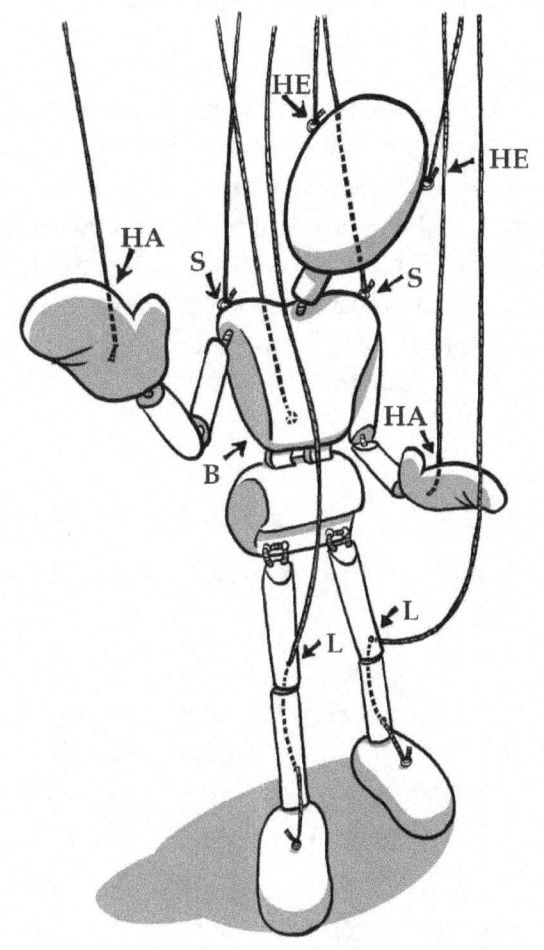

With these strings a marionette is capable of a wide range of movement, but not maximum movement. With this stringing the head is the only body part where maximum control of the movement is possible.

4 Designing a Marionette

The whole process of designing a marionette from character sketches to mechanical drawings is too big of a topic for this little book, but a few ideas are worth mentioning. Start your design process by drawing little sketches of the character you want to make. Draw a lot! If you think that you can't draw, you have all the more reason to draw a lot. Try to capture at least the essence of your future character.

Designing a puppet is a process of exaggeration and elimination.

Rarely do you want a puppet to be a naturalistic representation of a human being or animal. Some details of the appearance will need to be exaggerated and some will need to be eliminated. The same is true for the joints.

Part of the design process is deciding how the marionette should move, what parts of the marionette should move and what types of joints to use to achieve that movement. A roly-poly character may not need a waist joint. A ballerina on pointe may not need ankle joints. A stylized deer may move better without knee joints.

In the design phase you should also think about the range of movement of each joint. If a character needs to be able to sit down on its heels, the range of motion of the knee joints will need to accommodate the top of the thigh moving all the way to the heel. For a toy soldier, a hip joint with no twist will work well for marching. A dancer will probably need a looser hip joint.

You will need to decide what joints and what range of movement are needed by your character. A figure with more joints will need more strings to control the movement, which leads to more complicated controls and more difficult manipulation.

More moving parts isn't better, if you can't control the movement.

I would much rather see a simple marionette moving well than a complicated marionette moving poorly or barely moving at all.

5 Joints

The purpose of a joint is to connect two parts of a marionette, but more specifically to determine what movement is allowed and prevented. Should the movement be restricted to a single plane, like a hinge will do? Should twist be allowed? What should the range of motion be? In other words, how much movement in a particular direction should be allowed? When considering the different types of joints to choose from the focus should be on how the movement is restricted.

Most joints used for marionettes fit into one of a few categories.

Single Point Joint

A single point joint connects two parts at essentially a single point. It allows movement in all directions and allows twist. A single point joint is usually used for neck

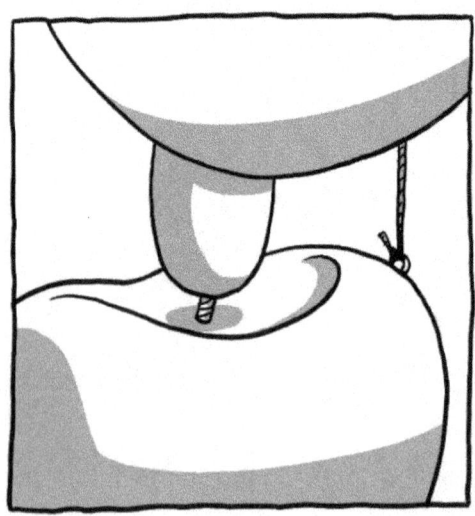

and shoulder joints and sometimes for wrist joints. A ball and socket joint is a type of single point joint. A single cord can be used as a very effective single point joint.

For a neck joint, however, it is useful to restrict the amount of twist that is allowed. The marionette shouldn't look more than about 90° in either direction. Using an eye screw sunk into the base of the neck and a loop of cord allows the twist movement to be restricted.

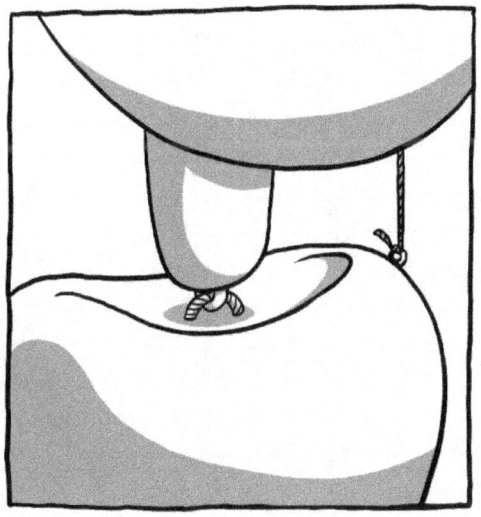

By restricting the movement of a joint to the desired range of motion the puppeteer is freed up from having to manage the range of motion through manipulation and can focus more attention on performance.

Hinge Joint

A hinge joint allows movement in only one plane and doesn't allow twist. Hinge joints are usually used for elbow, knee, ankle and sometimes wrist. One type of hinge joint is a cord joint where two cords go through holes on the edges of two pieces of wood. The two cords prevent the joint from twisting. The diagrams below show a cord joint being constructed and a completed joint.

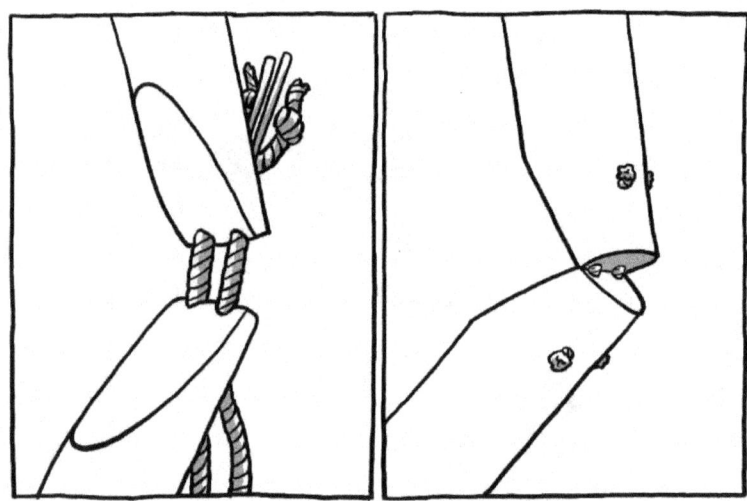

Tongue and groove is another type of hinge joint. The tongue on one piece fits into the groove on the other piece. The joint pivots on a pin that goes through holes in both pieces.

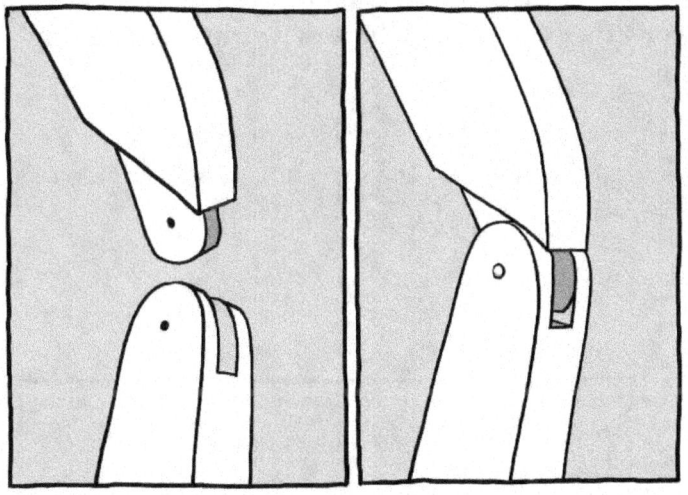

A tongue and groove joint is a good choice if the joint will not be covered by a costume.

Loose Hinge Joint

As the name implies, a loose hinge joint is a joint that is much looser than a traditional hinge joint. It will stay generally oriented in one direction, but it does allow some twist and side to side movement. A loose hinge joint may be constructed of a fabric tube or a strip of leather or nylon.

It is most often used for the hip joint. I like to use a cord through eye screws for the hip joint. It allows side to side movement as well as front to back.

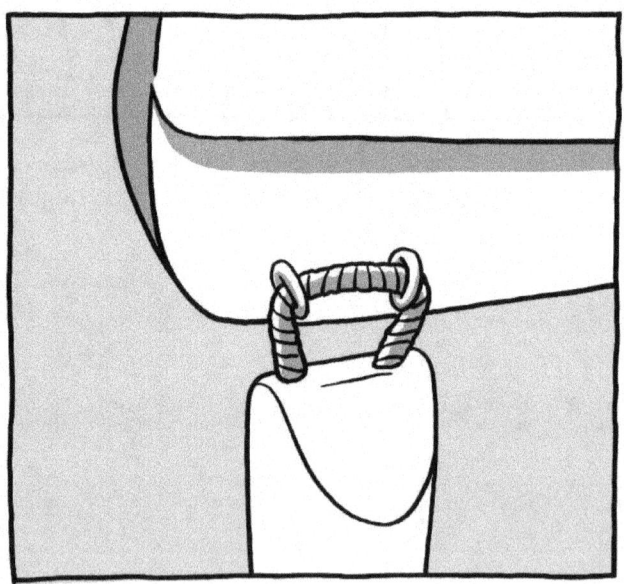

It will also continue to maintain orientation in one plane without twisting when the hip is tilted.

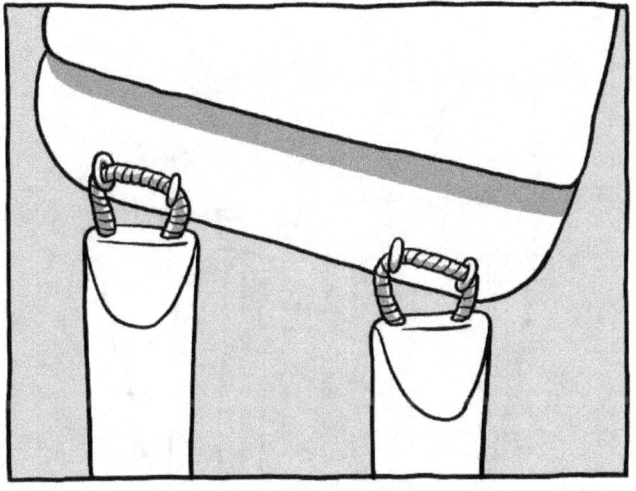

Combination Joint

A combination joint is actually two separate joints used in combination. A turnbuckle hip joint is an example.

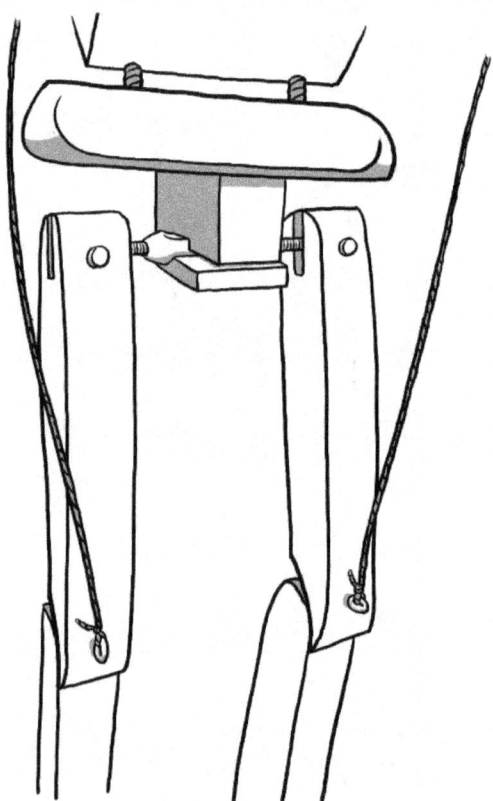

The center of the turnbuckle is fixed to the hip. The thigh is attached to the turnbuckle with a dowel that goes through the top of the leg and through the eye of the eye bolt.

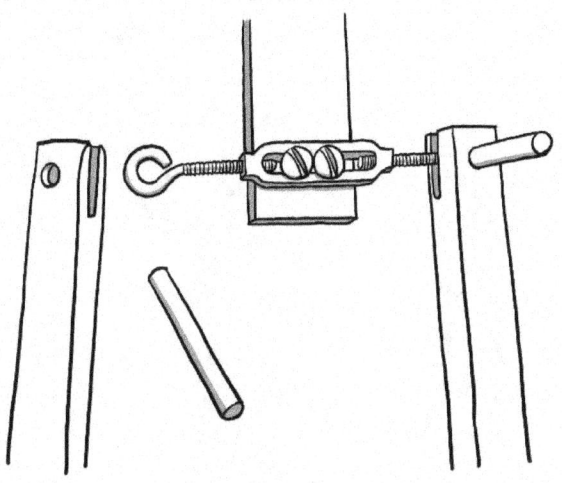

The forward and back movement of the leg is achieved by the rotation of the eye bolt thread in the turnbuckle. The sideways movement is achieved by the dowel rotating within the eye.

What sets the turnbuckle hip joint apart from other hip joints is that it does not allow any twist. **The movement that is not allowed makes the turnbuckle hip joint effective.**

Joint Stops

To allow the correct range of motion, a joint must have stops built into it. A joint without stops will overextend.

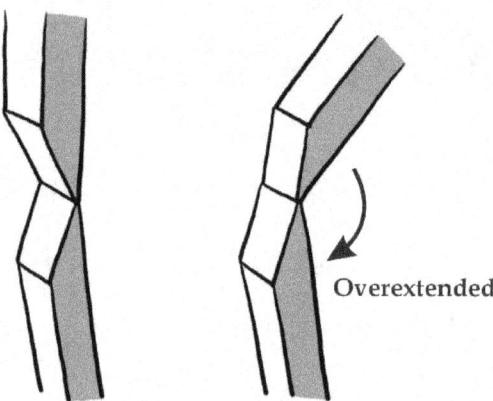

Overextended

A stop can be hard or soft. A hard stop will have two surfaces that come into contact with each other to prevent further movement. Such as:

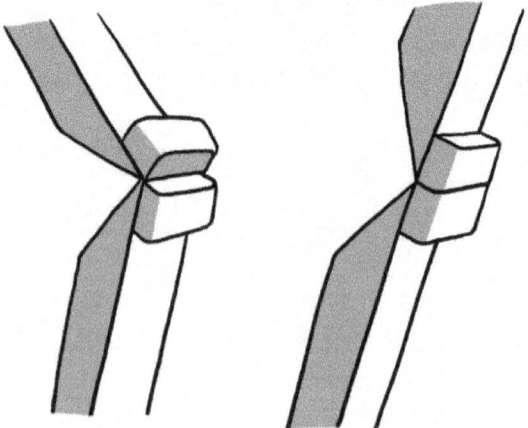

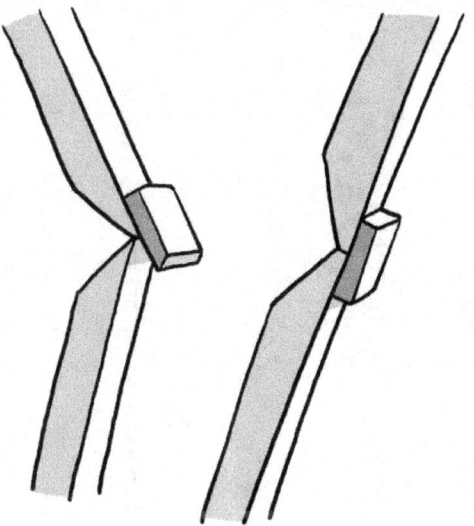

A soft stop uses a soft, flexible material (cord, fabric, etc.) to limit the movement of a joint.

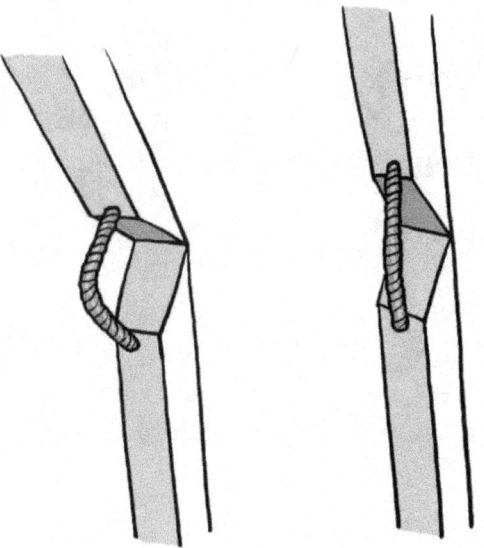

Stops for tongue and groove joints are very similar. The interior of the tongue and groove joints are shown to more clearly show the stops.

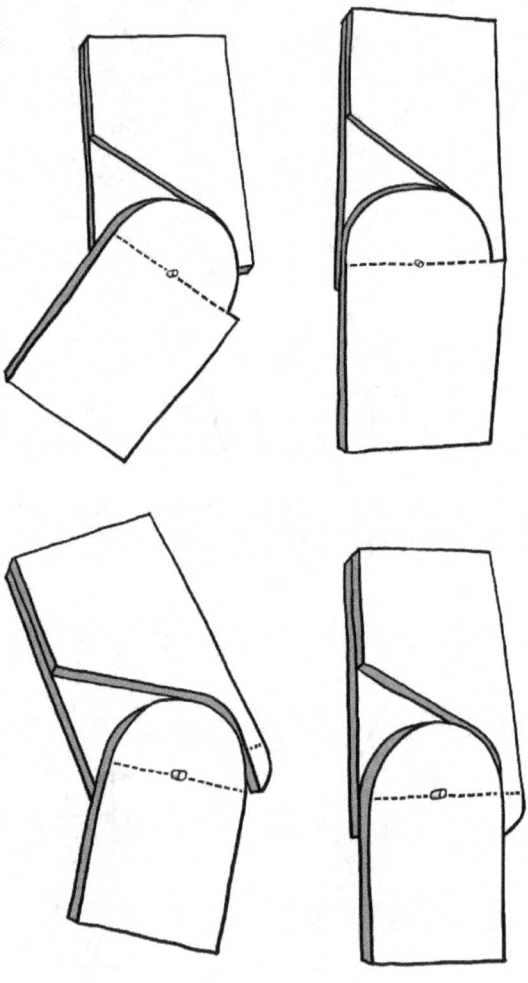

6 Where do the strings go?

The strings on a marionette really serve two purposes:

1) Support (holding the marionette stable)
2) Control (allowing the marionette to move when strings are moved)

The shoulder and back strings are generally for support. The head strings provide a combination of support and control. The leg and hand strings provide control. The placement of each string is determined by its purpose.

When determining the placement of the head strings, the weight distribution in the head has to be considered. Usually, the head strings are placed slightly above the ears, but you have to be sure that the placement doesn't allow the head to fall backwards.

As shown in the next diagram, when the shoulder strings are slack, the head strings will take all of the weight of the marionette. The weight of the body will be pulling down on the head at the neck joint. In this position the weight of the portion of the head in front of the head strings should be greater than the weight of the portion behind the head strings. This is so the head will fall forward when the shoulder strings are tightened and start to support some of the weight of the body.

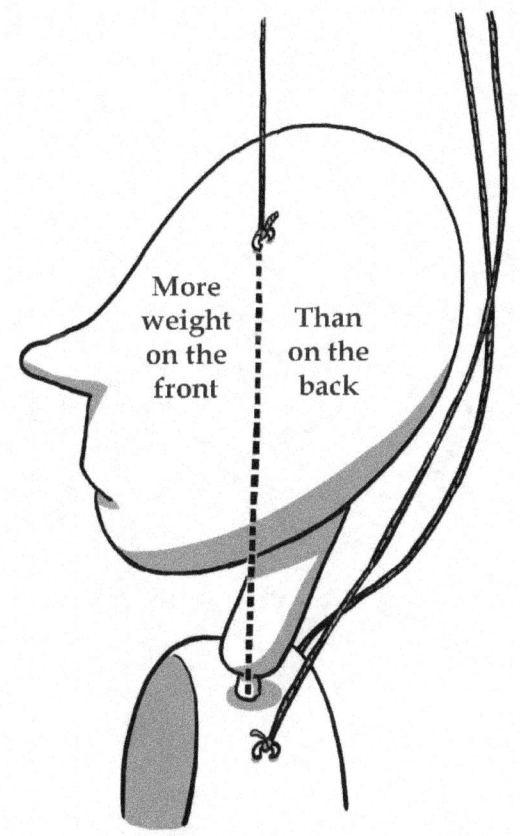

More weight on the front

Than on the back

If the head falls backwards, the head strings should be moved a little bit towards the back of the head.

Placement of the hand string will affect the "at rest" positions of the hands. If the wrist joint is a hinge joint, the placement will affect the "at rest" angle between the hand and the forearm. If the wrist joint is a single point joint, the placement will also affect whether the palms face down, up or somewhere in between.

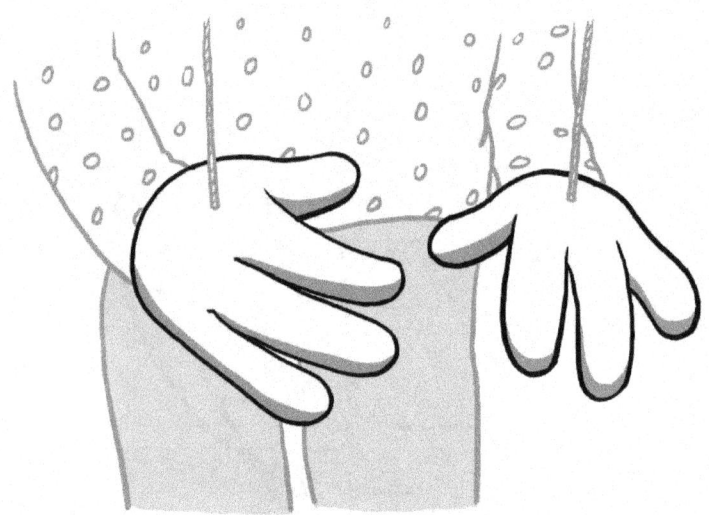

Placement of the nine basic strings is relatively straight forward. Placement of additional strings may take more trial and error. Strings are sometimes added to the elbows, wrists, heels, calves and chest. Facial animation will require additional strings. Additional hand strings can be used to gain greater control and a wider range of motion.

Additional strings may also make a marionette harder to manipulate. You can lose the ability to perform spontaneously if the stringing becomes too complex. Strings can interfere with each other as more strings are added. As the marionette moves, a specialty string may become taut and prevent movement or it may get in the way of an arm, a leg or another string.

Sooner or later as you add strings to a marionette to add specific movements, each new string added will also eliminate the possibility of other movement.

7 Finishing

Costuming, painting, hair and the other tasks necessary to finish the look of your marionette are also much too involved for this little book, but a few things are worth touching on.

If the back of the head is too heavy, the head will have a tendency to fall backwards. A heavy wig can lead to this problem, so the weight of any hair should be carefully considered. When choosing the material for hair avoid materials that may catch the strings.

A well designed and constructed costume can do a lot to establish the character of your marionette, but a poorly constructed costume or one made of stiff fabric can become a straitjacket on an otherwise flexible marionette. Consider where seams are placed, so that they don't add stiffness. Choose light, supple fabrics that move well. If your marionette will wear pants, learn what a gusset is and consider using one at the crotch to add extra fabric. A gusset can also be useful at the armpit.

Think about how much of the costume is really needed. Can some of it be suggested? If a shirt is partially covered by a coat, you may be able to only construct what will be seen, such as a collar and cuffs. Socks and tights can be painted on. Eliminate as much of the costume as you have to to get the movement that you need.

8 Controls

The first purpose of a control for a marionette is to
organize the strings. Generally, one of the puppeteer's
hands will hold the body of the control and the other hand
will be used to hold any removable bars and to grab
individual strings. One goal of control design is usually to
control as much of the marionette's movement as possible
by moving the body of the control and to minimize the
need to grab individual strings. Marionette controls vary
widely, but most will fall into one of the following
categories.

In the examples that follow, the strings are identified as
HE = head, HA = Hand, S = Shoulder, L = Leg, B = Back.

- Horizontal (airplane control, paddle control)

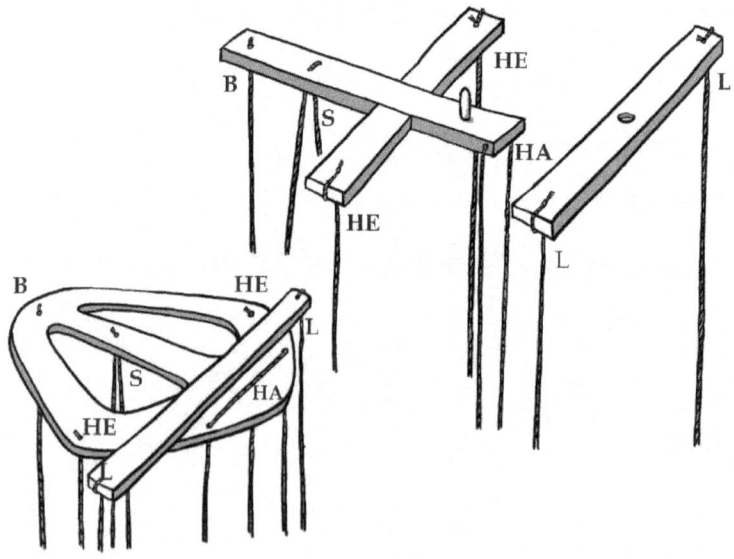

- Upright Control

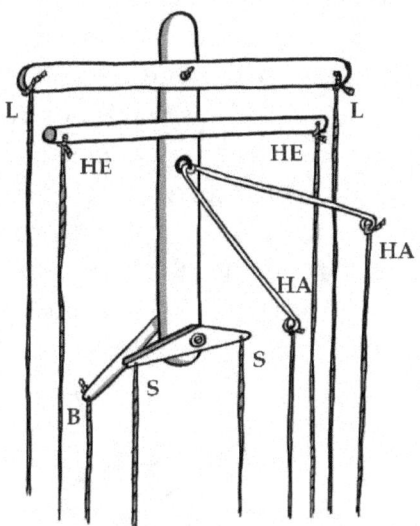

- Angled

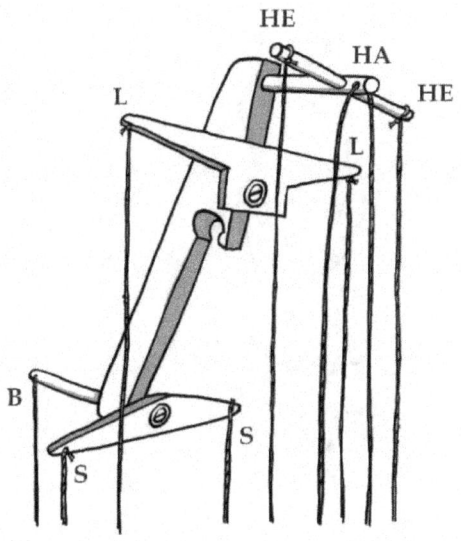

Although these three types of controls seem quite different, they have some very important similarities. On each of these controls the head strings attach to a bar that is rigidly fixed to the body of the control. The shoulder strings either are attached to the control at a single point or are attached to a separate bar that is not rigidly fixed to the body of the control. This arrangement allows the head movement, which is particularly important, to be controlled by moving the body of the control, but without causing the shoulder strings to move. For clarity, only the head strings are shown in the next drawing.

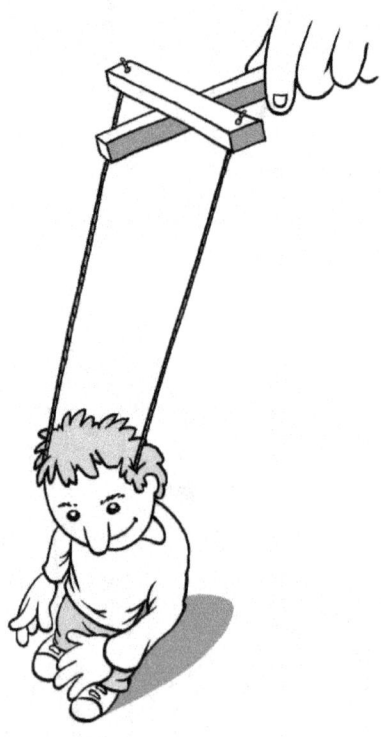

Another similarity is the general arrangement of the strings. The shoulder and back strings attach to the control behind the head strings. The leg and hand strings are at the very front of each control.

The size of the control is based on the size of the marionette. A rule of thumb is that the head bar should be 1 ½ times the width of the head, so if the head is 4 inches wide, the head bar should be at least 6 inches long. All the other dimensions primarily affect how much the control will need to move to get a particular movement. If the leg bar is short, you will have to rotate it more to lift leg the same distance that you would with a longer leg bar. In general a little bit bigger is better than a little too small.

9 Stringing

There are many different and affective approaches to stringing a marionette. I will mention a few ideas that have worked well for me.

The string that I use is black, braided, dacron or nylon fishing line. I prefer 15 or 20 lb. test. I rarely go heavier than 30 lb.

I generally will tie a string to the puppet and then adjust the length at the control. At the control I use 1/16" holes in the control and temporarily hold the strings in place with a round toothpick jammed into the hole from the top, while I adjust the length. I can very quickly and easily remove the toothpick, while holding the string in place and change the length of the string slightly before putting the toothpick back in place. When I am happy with the length of a string or pair of strings, I will tie off the string(s), remove the toothpicks and move on to the next strings.

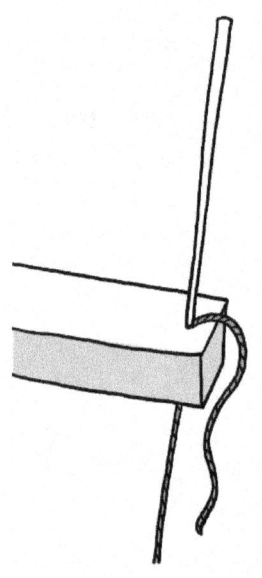

I used to use a needle with a large eye to feed the fishing line through the hole in the control, but I have recently discovered a product called "floss threaders." They are very thin pieces of flexible plastic with a loop forming a

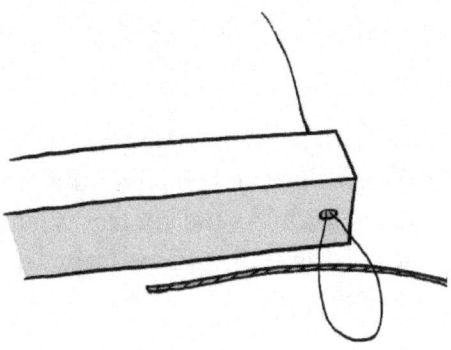

large eye on one end. They are meant for threading dental floss through tight spots between teeth, but they are ideal for the way that I string marionettes.

I like to clamp the control to a stand, so that the control is level and parallel with the ground. If you can't find a stand, a patient friend can hold the control level for you.

The order that I string is:

1) **Head** - Establish the height of the control above the ground, when the marionette is standing on the ground upright. It is generally comfortable for the puppeteer if the control is roughly at the puppeteer's elbow height.

2) **Shoulders** - Adjusting the length of the shoulder strings in relationship to the length of the head strings will determine the "at rest" position of the head.

3) **Legs** - I use a removable leg bar and after the leg strings are strung, I take the leg bar off of the control and set it on the ground, so that I can't accidentally string the hand strings through the leg strings.
4) **Hands** - I use a continuous string for the hand strings, so the string is tied at one hand, threaded through a hole in the control, then tied at the other hand.
5) **Back** - I generally string the back string, so that there is a little slack when the control is parallel to the ground. As the control is leaned forward, the back string will become tight and the puppet will also lean forward.

When using dacron or nylon fishing line, the last step is to put a small drop of glue on each knot, so that the knot won't untie itself. A white glue will work, but I usually use Duco Cement ™.

10 Hazards

The strings are both the blessing and the curse of
marionettes. The strings allow a marionette great visual
separation from the puppeteer, which gives them a
magical independence. The strings can also get caught on
anything in their way, which is much less magical.

The fingers of a marionette are a very common hazard.
Leg strings love to slide between fingers, which creates
problems for both the leg and hand movement. This
hazard can be prevented by running guard strings
between the fingers.

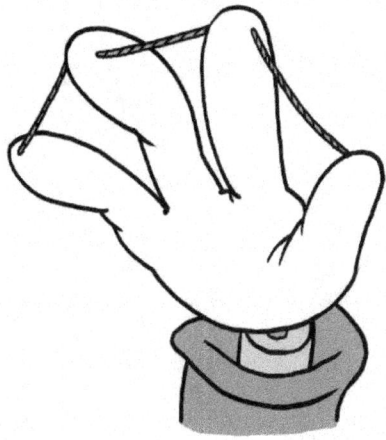

Guard strings can also be used to prevent strings from
getting caught in tongue and groove joints, buttons on
costumes, etc.

Beware the Eye Screw

Although eye screws have many uses when building marionettes and their controls, they can also create hazards, if not used carefully.

An eye screw on a marionette or control with an eye that is slightly open can catch a string in a way that is almost impossible to correct during performance.

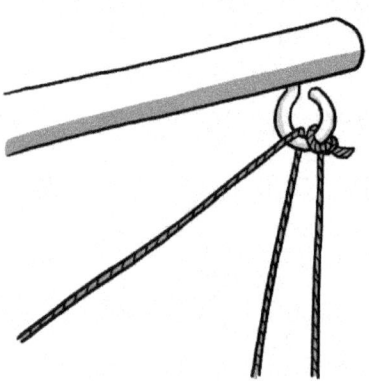

Side Note

Never use a pliers to screw in an eye screw that will have contact with string. A pliers can scratch the surface of the eye screw and create small, sharp burs, which over time can cut through the string running through the eye screw. Instead, I insert a round toothpick into the eye screw for leverage when screwing it in.

In many cases an eye screw on a control can be replaced with a hole drilled through some part of the control.

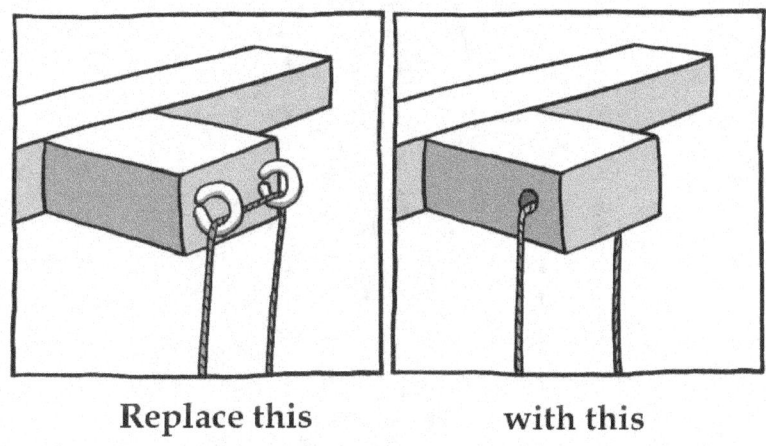

Replace this   with this

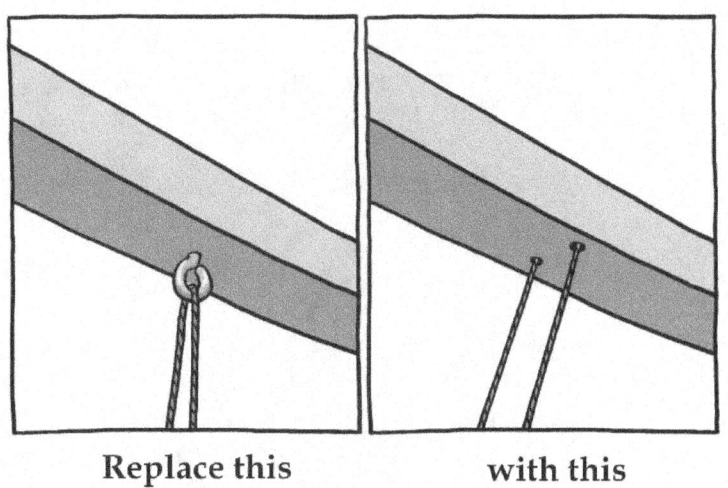

Replace this   with this

Even an eye screw with a tightly closed eye can catch a string around its shaft such as the eye screw on the head shown below.

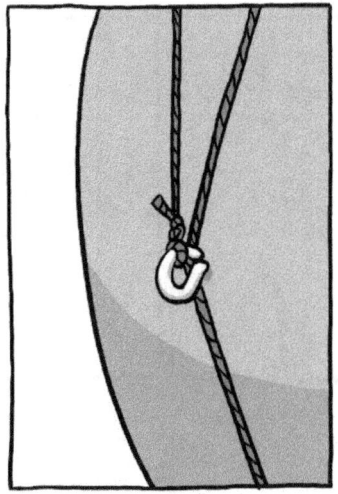

An eye screw that is sunk halfway will not be a hazard to strings.

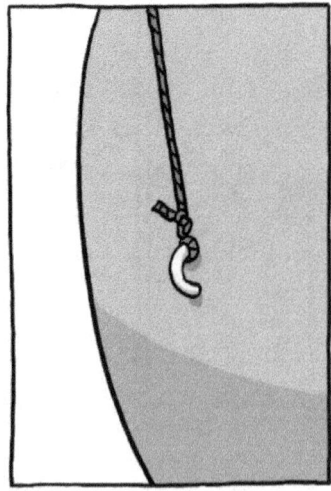

Some books will show interlocking eye screws used for marionette joints. However, if the eye screws twist in the wood, the joint will move in the wrong direction. These joints can also be noisy. In the worst case, if the joined parts rotate too far, the eye screws can lock.

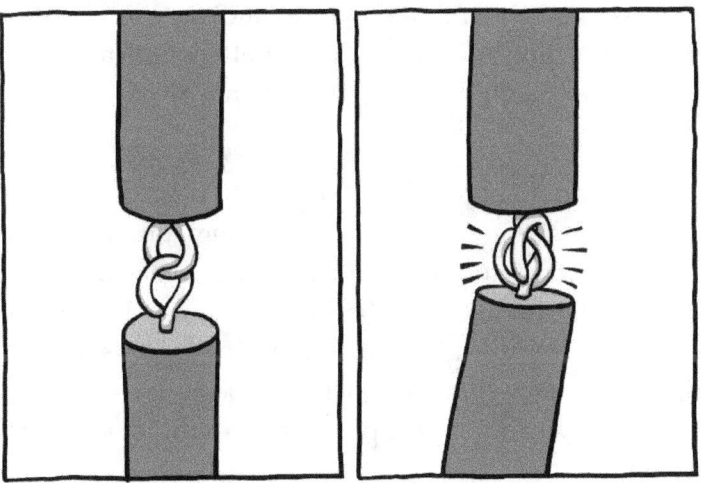

There is usually a better choice of joint than interlocking eye screws.

11 Make It Move / Let It Move

When I started building marionettes my focus was on what I could make a marionette do. Although I still carefully plan the movement that I want when building a marionette, today I am much more interested in discovering what a particular marionette wants to do. Here are a few thoughts about how to approach a new marionette.

Start by holding your marionette in the air and slowly lowering it to the ground without looking at it. Feel when its feet touch the ground and its legs start to support some of its weight. Get used to what this feels like. This is the upright posture position of your marionette. It is the position that you will come back to, so you want to be able to feel when you are in this position without looking.

Start with your marionette standing still. Tilt and twist the control so that the head lowers slightly and looks to one side. Lift an arm and gesture in the direction that the puppet is looking. Try different shapes of gestures. Try the same gesture at different speeds. Work in front of a mirror, so that you can see what each movement conveys.

Holding the leg bar at the very center of the bar, tilt the bar to lift a leg string and take a step forward. Try another step. The body of the marionette will need to drop slightly with each step forward and then come back up as the feet come together. Walking will be the most difficult movement at first, so take your time and don't get frustrated.

Using breath to establish the life of a puppet has become a prevalent idea within puppetry, but the physical appearance of breathing is not as central when working with marionettes. As with all puppets, you should pay close attention to your marionette's focus at all times. Where is it looking? **Focus conveys thought.** What the puppet is looking at or trying to avoid looking at or intentionally looking away from will tell the audience what it is thinking.

In an improv class about developing characters, I learned the phrase "How you do what you do is who you are." In other words, movement conveys character. Is the movement slow? Fast? Abrupt? Smooth? Gentle? Violent? **In the end, movement should convey character and emotion.**

When you design and build a marionette, you generally have very specific ideas in mind. You are creating a character and you want that character to be able to do certain things and move in certain ways. As you work with your completed marionette, you will tend to focus on the movement that you planned from the beginning, but you need to also be open to the surprises that will inevitably come with a new marionette. Those surprises will only appear, if you take the time to explore, to play.

Marionettes love architecture and furniture (stairs, walls, chairs, boxes ...), something to lean against, stand on, hide behind, sit on and explore. You'll discover lots of interesting movement, when you give your marionette a small playground to explore.

Your marionette may not do everything that you had hoped, but it will probably do things that you hadn't imagined.

12 Untangling

Marionettes do get tangled. The more you work with them the less it happens. Tangling usually only happens when strings are slack, so avoid letting strings go completely slack during performance and hang the control up so that tension is kept on the strings when not in use.

Here are a few steps that will get you through even the worst tangles.

- Don't panic. Trying to untangle a marionette too quickly can create a major tangle from a minor tangle.
- Look at the control. Are any strings where they shouldn't be, such as wrapped over the control or caught on part of the control?
- Look at the puppet. Are any strings where they shouldn't be, such as wrapped around a limb?
- If there are any removeable bars on the control, such as a leg bar, untangle that bar from the rest of the strings and set it away from the other strings.
- Focus on untangling one string. The back string is a good choice. Untangle that one string between the control and the marionette. Most of the time that will untangle the whole marionette or nearly so.

13 Conclusions

Well, that's it. If you didn't know how to build or manipulate marionettes when you started this book, you probably still don't. However, I hope you will learn to build marionettes and discover how they move and fall in love with them. Hopefully this book will be helpful on that journey. I initially learned about marionettes from library books, because there were no puppeteers in my corner of the world. Books and online tutorials can be a good place to get more details. I have listed a few particularly good books in the bibliography.

As I mentioned in the introduction, I do suggest starting simple. Attach a string to a wooden ball and just get used to how it moves through the air. Albrecht Roser designed the scarf marionette as a teaching tool. You should be able to find scarf marionette instructions online, if you can't, then send me an email.

The best way to learn marionettes is in person, hands on from another puppeteer. I teach classes and do mentoring in the Minneapolis area and have taught at the O'Neill Puppetry Conference. If you need help finding puppeteers working with marionettes in your area, let me know and I'll see if I can help.

My hope is that this book will be a resource that you can come back to as you acquire more knowledge and experience about marionettes. If you have questions, insights or feedback, I'd love to hear them. You can contact me at:

kurt@huntermarionettes.com

14 Bibliography

Stevens, Martin. *Stevens' Course in Puppetry*. Charlemagne Press, 1997. (A great beginning to end book on creating a puppet show with three chapters on designing and building marionettes.)

Dwiggins, W. A. *Marionette in Motion*. Puppetry Imprints, 1939. (Reprinted by The Puppeteers of America in 1989. This booklet describes Dwiggins' principle of the counter balanced marionette.)

Beaton, Mabel and Les. *The Complete Book of Marionettes*. Dover Publications, 2011. (Originally published in 1948 as Marionettes: A Hobby for Everyone. A very good comprehensive resource.)

Coad, Luman. *Marionette Sourcebook: Theory and Technique*. Charlemagne Press, 1993. (The most comprehensive compilation of controls, jointing, etc.)

Roberts, John. *Carve a Marionette: A step by step guide*. 2018. (A well-illustrated, step by step guide to carving a marionette.)

Roberts, John. *Making Simple Marionettes*. The Crowood Press, 2019. (A well-illustrated guide mostly focused on simple marionettes.)

www.ingramcontent.com/pod-product-compliance
Lightning Source LLC
Chambersburg PA
CBHW071546120626
46550CB00006B/2596